BOOKER T. WASHINGTON

"Character Is Power"

Anne Schraff

Series Consultant:
Dr. Russell L. Adams, Chairman
Department of
Afro-American Studies,
Howard University

Enslow Publishers, Inc.
40 Industrial Road
Box 398
Berkeley Heights, NJ 07922
USA
http://www.enslow.com

"CHARACTER IS POWER."
—*Booker T. Washington*

Library of Congress Cataloging-in-Publication Data

Schraff, Anne E.
    Booker T. Washington : "character is power" / by Anne Schraff.
      p. cm. — (African-American biography library)
    Includes bibliographical references and index.
    ISBN 0-7660-2535-7
    1. Washington, Booker T., 1856–1915—Juvenile literature. 2. African Americans—
Biography—Juvenile literature. 3. Educators—United States—Biography—Juvenile
literature. 4. Character—Case studies—Juvenile literature. I. Title. II. Series.
    E185.97.W4S235 2005
    370.92—dc22

                                  2005034880

Printed in the United States of America

10 9 8 7 6 5 4 3 2 1

Illustration Credits: Enslow Publishers, Inc., p. 113; Hemera Technologies, Inc., p. 32;
Library of Congress, pp. 4, 6, 13, 16, 17, 19, 22, 26, 28, 30, 34, 39, 44, 48, 50, 55, 57, 61, 64, 65,
68, 71, 75, 79, 83, 86, 88, 92, 100, 107, 108, 111; National Archives, p. 81; Northwind Picture
Archives, pp. 10, 11; Special Collections and Archives, W.E.B. Du Bois Library, University of
Massachusetts Amherst, p. 94.

Cover Illustrations: Library of Congress (both)

Contents

Booker Taliaferro Washington

Chapter 1

Boy on Fire

Sixteen-year-old Booker T. Washington started out on a five-hundred-mile journey one day in October 1872. While working in a West Virginia coal mine, he had heard two men talking about a school in Virginia where poor boys and girls could work to pay their tuition. The school was Hampton Institute, and the minute he heard about it, Booker wanted to go there. He later recalled, "I was on fire constantly with one ambition, and that was to go to Hampton."[1]

Booker's mother wanted what was best for her son, but she described his journey to Hampton as "a wild goose chase."[2] Booker did not even have enough money to get all the way there. On the day he left Malden, West Virginia, his friends and family came to wish him well. Booker was given whatever small gifts the local people could afford. Some gave him a quarter or a nickel, while others gave him a handkerchief.

Booker carried one small suitcase and enough money to go part of the way by train. He boarded the newly built Chesapeake and Ohio Railroad at Charleston Station and rode until his money just about ran out. With the few coins he had left, he took a stagecoach another hundred miles. At night the stagecoach stopped at a hotel, and all the passengers got off. Booker joined the stream of people entering the hotel, but when he reached the door he was

Booker traveled by foot, by train, and by stagecoach.

Segregation

After the Civil War put an end to slavery, a system of racial segregation appeared in the South. African Americans were excluded from hotels, restaurants, and other public places that were open to white people only. It was difficult for African-American travelers to find places to eat or sleep. They had to look for all-black establishments that would serve them.

stopped. He was the only African-American passenger, and he was not permitted to sleep in the hotel. It was a cold night and Booker spent it walking around to keep warm.

The next day, a tired Booker continued his journey on foot. He had no more money for transportation, but sometimes a sympathetic wagon driver would give him a ride for a few miles. When he finally reached Richmond, Virginia, Booker was still eighty-two miles from Hampton Institute. He stopped at several hotels, hoping to exchange work for a night's lodging, but he was turned down everywhere.

Cold and hungry, Booker spent another night outside. He walked the streets of Richmond, passing many food stands that sold fried chicken and apple pies. "It seemed to me," Booker later said, "that I would have promised all that I expected to possess in the future to have gotten hold of one of those chicken legs or one of those pies."[3]

Near midnight, Booker grew so tired that he crawled under a raised-plank sidewalk and stretched out on the ground with his suitcase for a pillow. As he tried to sleep, he heard people walking overhead.

In the morning, Booker saw a ship unloading cargo on the docks. The ship's captain allowed him to help unload pig iron—raw iron that has been melted and then molded into small block shapes—in exchange for enough money to buy breakfast. "About the best breakfast that I have ever eaten," Booker later remembered.[4] With fresh energy, the boy walked the rest of the way to Hampton. He arrived there needing a shave, a haircut, and a bath. His clothing was filthy. School was already under way, and one student called Booker "an innocent green looking rustic West Virginia boy."[5]

The head teacher at Hampton looked at the ragged, dirty boy and hesitated to accept him as a student. She then asked him to clean a classroom to show what he could do.[6] Booker knew how to clean a room well. He swept it three times and dusted it four times. Booker later said, "The sweeping of that room was my college examination."[7] The teacher checked the room thoroughly, wiping her white handkerchief on all the tables and benches. Then she turned to Booker and said, "I guess we will try you as a student."[8]

"I felt that I had reached the promised land," Booker T. Washington said of that day.[9]

Chapter 2

Childhood

round April 5, 1856, a baby boy named Booker Taliaferro was born on James Burrough's farm just outside Hale's Ford, Virginia.[1] The mother was a slave known as Jane. Her first son, John, was four years old. Booker was born on top of a mound of rags piled on the dirt floor of his mother's cabin. Jane's half-sister, Sophia, acted as midwife, delivering the baby. Booker had reddish hair and glowing gray eyes. His father was a white man, but Booker was never to know the man's name. "Whoever he was," Booker later said, "I never heard of his taking the least interest in me or providing in any way for my rearing."[2]

Shortly after Booker's birth, his mother married a slave named Washington Ferguson. Booker's sister, Amanda, was born in 1859. The family now consisted of two boys and a girl.

Hale's Ford was a community of small farms in the Blue Ridge Mountain region. The white farmers of

Booker was born in this log cabin.

the region owned a few slaves and worked alongside them in the fields, planting and harvesting tobacco, grains, wheat, corn, oats, potatoes, beans, and greens.

Booker's owner, James Burroughs, had more than one hundred acres in Franklin County. He and his wife, Elizabeth, lived in a five-room house surrounded by a picket fence. There were two one-room slave cabins behind the house. Hogs wandered freely on the land, living off acorns and chestnuts. Burroughs owned four horses, four cow, sand some sheep. He had ten or eleven slaves, including Booker's family.

The cabin where Booker was born was built of split oak logs. The single room was fourteen by sixteen feet. A narrow door swung in the wind on rusty hinges. The windows were just openings in the walls without screens or glass. Wooden shutters closed out the air and light in the winter. In the summer insects came in at will. In the center of the room there was a hole in the floor, where sweet potatoes were stored. Cracks in the walls were sealed with wet mud. When the mud hardened it often fell out. Booker's mother

The cabin had only one room.

owned a cat, and the holes in the cabin walls were so big that often the cat used them to come in and go out.

Booker's mother spent most of her day cooking for the Burroughs family and the other slaves. Laura Burroughs, a daughter, described Jane as "our cook, and by the way a good one," adding that "she was neat and brisk."[3] Booker's mother was too busy working to spend much time with her children, but she was affectionate with them when she had a little free time. Booker later recalled that he and his brother never sat down to eat at a table. They ate what they could snatch from the kitchen fire—the Burroughs family leftovers of cornbread, potatoes, and a few scraps of meat. One of Booker's memories was of his mother cooking a chicken late at night and then waking her children for a midnight feast. He never knew where she got the chicken.

There was very little play in Booker's childhood, other than an occasional run through the fruit trees and willow trees with his brother and the other slave children. Booker's days were usually filled with chores. An exception to the dreary routine was Christmas. Booker later said that "Christmas was the great event of the whole year to the slaves throughout the South."[4] The work stopped for a week, and on Christmas day each slave got a gift. One Christmas, Booker awoke at four in the morning to find his Christmas

> There was very little play in Booker's childhood.

stocking brimming with red candy and six ginger cakes. But the best gift he ever received was a pair of little wooden shoes with leather tops. Booker was eight years old, and these were his first shoes. They were hard to walk in, but the hickory-wood soles kept his feet warm and dry.

One of young Booker's jobs on the farm was to stand at

This slave family lived in South Carolina in the mid-1800s. Booker said his childhood was typical of many young slaves.

◆ ◆ ◆ ◆ ◆

Slave Codes

During slavery it was strictly forbidden to teach a slave to read or write or even to give them books or newspapers to look at. Keeping slaves uneducated was seen as a way to keep them from dreaming of a better life—and perhaps rebelling or escaping.

the Burroughs' dinner table and fan the flies away from their food as they ate. When he was older, he had to make a three-mile trip on horseback, delivering a heavy bag of corn to the mill to be ground into cornmeal. The boy climbed on the horse, and a man lifted the bag across the horse, then Booker began his journey. One day the load of corn shifted and fell off the horse. Booker was too small to get it back up, so he sat beside the road, hoping some kindly soul would come along to lift the sack back onto the horse. He waited a long time before a stranger helped him. Because of the delay, he had to ride home in the darkness, a terrifying trip for the small boy.

As a child, the only clothing Booker owned was a coarse, homemade flax shirt. It was so stiff that it chafed his skin painfully. When Booker got a new shirt, his older brother volunteered to wear it for a while until it was broken in and not so stiff. Booker always remembered this act of kindness from his older brother because the new flax fibers had been so hard on his young skin.

Booker himself was not cruelly treated on the Burroughs' farm, but one day his uncle committed a minor misdeed and the boy saw him punished. Booker's uncle was stripped naked, tied to a tree, and whipped with rawhide. The incident remained with Booker throughout his life.

Booker had no schooling as a child, but sometimes he was given the task of carrying books for the Burroughs children as they went to school. Once there, Booker would take a moment to peer into the classroom where the white children disappeared. He watched them sitting at desks and opening those books he carried for them. Later he recalled, "I had the feeling that to get into a schoolhouse and study in this way would be about the same as getting into paradise."[5]

Booker's stepfather escaped from slavery during the Civil War. He ran off one night and Booker was awakened in the morning to hear his mother praying loudly for the success of President Abraham Lincoln's army. Booker did not understand what the Civil War was about, but he did see young white men marching by in uniforms. His mother explained to him that President Lincoln had issued a document called the Emancipation Proclamation and that maybe one day soon all the slaves would be free.

It was not until April 1865 that the slaves on the Burroughs

> "I had the feeling that to get into a schoolhouse . . . would be about the same as getting into paradise."

Emancipation Proclamation

On January 1, 1863, President Abraham Lincoln issued the Emancipation Proclamation. It freed all the slaves in

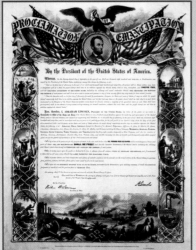

the southern states that were rebelling against the United States. It did not free all the slaves in the country. The Civil War had to end before that would happen. All the slaves were declared free by the passage of the Thirteenth Amendment to the U.S. Constitution in December

The Emancipation Proclamation 1865. It stated that neither slavery nor involuntary servitude would exist within the United States.

farm learned that they were free. All the slaves living in the area were told to gather in front of the Burroughs's house. An officer from the Union Army read the Emancipation Proclamation to the crowd of forty to fifty slaves. Booker said later that he realized at that moment that this document "made us men instead of property."[6] The slaves were told they were now free to leave their masters. Booker stood beside his mother, who leaned over and kissed her children, tears of joy streaming down her face.

Booker's family had been freed, but they had no money and nowhere to go. So they remained on the Burroughs farm. Life went on the same as before until they received word that Booker's stepfather was now working at a salt furnace in Kanawha County, West Virginia. He told his wife and stepchildren to come and join him. In August

Union soldiers traveled around the South
telling slaves that they were now free.

1865, the family left the Burroughs farm and set out in a two-horse wagon on the two-hundred-mile journey to West Virginia. Booker's mother had asthma and heart trouble, so she rode in the wagon with six-year-old Amanda. Booker and John walked most of the way. They camped each night in the open. It took them about two weeks to reach the small town of Malden, West Virginia.

Booker's family found Ferguson living in a cabin among a cluster of cabins very close together. Conditions in the settlement were terrible. Booker was sickened by the filth and garbage in and around the cabins. He was frightened by the rough, noisy behavior of the men who gambled, got drunk, and got into violent fights. The residents of the settlement included both blacks and whites. Most of the men worked in the Kanawha salt mine, where they processed salt for the pork-packing factories of Cincinnati, Ohio. The salt brine was boiled to a damp, solid state, then dried in a pan where it turned into the crystallized salt that was shoveled into barrels for shipping. Booker and John helped their stepfather with the heavy work of packing the salt. The workday began at 4 A.M. and continued until after dark. Although the boys worked hard, their stepfather kept all the money.

The black neighborhood of Malden was called Tinkersville. One day Booker saw a young man speaking to a crowd there. He was reading a newspaper to a group of adults who listened intently. None of them could read

Booker worked in a salt mine like this, shoveling salt into barrels.

or write. Booker envied the young man's ability to read. Booker's mother knew how her son longed to read and she scraped together enough money to buy him a copy of Webster's Blueback spelling book. Booker memorized the book.

Booker asked his stepfather to let him go to school, but he refused. Booker then asked the teacher at Tinkersville School, William Davis, to tutor him during adult sessions in the evenings. Finally Booker's stepfather relented and

> Booker envied the young man's ability to read.

allowed Booker to attend regular school as long as he worked in the salt mine from 4 A.M. to 9 A.M. and then again after school. Booker was delighted to be able to put in a full school day.

On the first day of school, each student was called on to give their name. Up until then, Booker did not use a last name. He was simply Booker. Hearing the other children calling out their last names, Booker blurted out "Booker Washington." Later he said of the day, "Not many men in our country have had the privilege of naming themselves in the way that I have."[7] From that day forward, Booker was Booker Washington. When he learned later on that soon after his birth his mother had given him the second name of Taliaferro, he added the middle initial *T*.

Booker's family appears in the U.S. Census of 1870 with the last name of Ferguson because Booker's stepfather was once owned by a family with that name, but neither Booker nor anyone else in the family besides his stepfather ever used the name Ferguson.

Booker noticed that all the other boys in the classroom wore caps but he had none. Nor did he have the money to buy one. When he told his mother of his problem, she sewed him a cap from pieces of homespun denim. It did not look like the store-bought caps, but Booker wore it proudly. He was so happy to be in school that nothing else mattered.

Later in life Booker recalled the joy he got from reading stories in school about poor boys who overcame their obstacles to become successful. "The trouble in my case," he said, "was that the stories we read in school were all concerned with the success and achievements of white boys and men."[8]

> Booker was so happy to be in school that nothing else mattered.

When the salt mines in Malden needed fewer men, Booked went to work in the coal mines. It was dirty, dangerous work. The miners had to walk a mile through underground tunnels from the mine opening to where the coal was being chopped from the walls. Sometimes Booker became lost in the mine when his lantern went out. There was the ever-present danger of falling rocks or explosions. One day in the mine, Booker overheard two young miners talking about a school—Hampton Normal and Agricultural Institute in Virginia. It was for black boys and girls. If they could not afford board and tuition, they were given jobs to work for their education. Hearing about this school filled Booker with fresh hope.

In 1867, when Booker was eleven, he got permission from his stepfather to work as a houseboy in town. Houseboys were domestic servants who did work such as cleaning and running errands. Booker would earn $5 a month, and he promised to give it all to his stepfather. Booker was eager to be out of the mines.

For Booker, as for these boys, working in a coal mine
was difficult and dangerous.

Booker went to work in the home of the upper-class
white family of General Lewis Ruffner, and his wife, Viola.
Ruffner owned the salt and coal mines in Malden and his
home was a nice wooden house overlooking a river. Viola
Ruffner was a very demanding woman who wanted everything done just right. Boys who worked for her usually did
not last long. Booker heard of Viola Ruffner's demand for
perfection, and he trembled with nervousness at the beginning. But very quickly the New England–born woman and

the boy bonded. She wanted the work done promptly and correctly, and she insisted on total honesty. Booker respected that. Later he said of the experience, "The lessons that I learned in the home of Mrs. Ruffner were as valuable to me as any education I have ever gotten anywhere since."[9]

Booker ran off soon after he started working for the Ruffners, becoming a cabin boy on a steamship traveling from Malden to Cincinnati. During the time he worked for Mrs. Ruffner he sometimes grew restless and left to spend time trying other jobs. But he always returned to Mrs. Ruffner. He loved and respected her. She reinforced his own ethic of hard work, cleanliness, and thrift, principles on which he would later build his philosophy of life.

"I was on fire constantly with one ambition, and that was to go to Hampton."[10]

While working as a houseboy for Mrs. Ruffner, Booker also attended school several hours a day. Booker took a dry-goods box and put shelves in it, and here he placed the few books he proudly possessed. Most were gifts from Mrs. Ruffner. Booker called the box "my 'library.'"[11]

Viola Ruffner told Booker stories of her own New England childhood, which had been poverty-stricken. She encouraged him by saying that she had risen above all that, and he could too. Mrs. Ruffner grew vegetables and grapes. She asked Booker to go from door-to-door selling the produce. Each morning the boy climbed on a wagon and traveled to the towns between Malden and Charleston, eight miles away. He visited the homes of miners, boatmen, and farmers, and sold all the produce. Booker brought home every penny. Viola Ruffner said of Booker, "his conduct has always been without fault."[12]

On December 4, 1869, violence erupted between a group of white men called Gideon's Band and some black men. Gideon's band, like the Ku Klux Klan, aimed to terrorize black people into submission. The next day, the agitation between the races continued. General Ruffner, hearing some gunshots not far from his home, ran out to help. As he tried to soothe both sides, someone threw a brick, hitting Ruffner in the head and knocking him unconscious. The fighting resumed, with hostile blacks and whites hurling rocks and bricks. For young Booker, who had come running out behind Ruffner, it was a horrifying eyewitness view of savage race hatred. Ruffner never fully recovered from the injury, and Booker never forgot the incident.

As Booker became a teenager, his dream of going to Hampton Institute became stronger with each passing day.

Chapter 3

From Student to Teacher

ampton Institute had been open for just four years when Booker T. Washington arrived there in October 1872. The school had one brick building, the three-story academic hall that served as living quarters for the boys and men as well as classrooms for all the students. The old Union Army barracks that housed the girls and women was also used as the dining hall for all the students. Booker's first reaction to the school was to call it "the largest and most beautiful building I had ever seen."[1]

The conditions at Hampton were rustic, with no table-cloths on the dining-room tables and no coffee cups. Instead, coffee was served in yellow bowls. Still, Hampton was a great improvement over life for many of the students, including Booker. Meals were served on a regular basis, and there were sheets on the beds. There were bathtubs and toothbrushes.

Most of the Hampton students were adult men and women. Some were as old as forty. Booker was one of the youngest.

A man who had a great influence on Booker's life was thirty-three-year-old General Samuel Chapman Armstrong, the head of Hampton Institute. Armstrong had been one of the youngest generals of the Civil War. He was a handsome, clean-shaven man later described by Booker T. Washington as "the most perfect specimen of man, physically, mentally, and spiritually," and "more than a father to me."[2] Armstrong was well-liked and respected by all the students, but he was especially significant in Booker's life. In a very real sense he was the father the boy never had.

General Armstrong

As a new student at Hampton, Booker was given the job of janitor to pay his board and tuition.

He liked the job because it gave him contact with the teachers, especially Armstrong. Throughout his time at Hampton, Booker performed janitorial work. He learned no other skilled trade.

At the end of the first school year, all the students went home for the summer and the school was closed. But Booker had no money for the trip home and his family had none to send him. He had to find another place to stay.

Booker wrote that he felt "sad and homesick" watching the other students packing their things for the trip home.[3] He finally found a job at a restaurant at Fortress Monroe, where his wages barely covered a room and food.

During his time at Hampton Institute, Booker developed the habit of reading the Bible not only for spiritual guidance, but also as literature. From then on, all through his life, he read daily from the Bible. Booker was also developing his public speaking skills. A teacher, Miss Nathalie Lord, gave Booker private lessons in breathing techniques, emphasis on important words, and pronunciation. Booker joined debating societies at Hampton to further improve his public speaking.

> "I had a good deal of boyish pride, and I tried to hide, as far as I could, from the other students the fact that I had no money and nowhere to go."[4]

These Hampton students were studying physics.

Enrollment grew rapidly at Hampton as word spread that the school offered a free education for young blacks who would work for it. Hampton became so crowded that tents were used for the overflow. Booker was one of the students who volunteered to live in a tent even though it was cold and miserable in the winter.

The school day at Hampton was twelve hours long, beginning with military drill at 5 A.M., followed by academic and vocational training and work. Students were expected to learn a skill that would enable them to make a living. Booker was already a skilled janitor so he took no additional training.

Hampton offered a secondary or high school education. There are no records of Washington's academic record there. Hampton did not keep good records. But Washington became a "Middler" (junior) in his second year, and a senior in his third year, graduating in three years. This indicates that he was a better than average student.

At the end of Booker's second year, gifts from his mother and brother made it possible for him to go home for the summer. He returned to Malden in the summer of 1874. He found economic conditions bad, with widespread unemployment. Booker searched without luck for a summer job. One night, after traveling a distance and looking for work all day, he was too tired to go home. He slept in an old abandoned house by the side of the road. His

Booker near the end of his teen years.

brother, John, went searching for him and finally found him. He told Booker the sad news that their mother had died that night. Booker later described hearing the news as "the saddest and blankest moment in my life."[5] Booker's mother had been in poor health for a long time, but Booker never thought she was this close to death when he left to look for work. Booker's grief was worsened by the fact that he had not been able to be at his mother's side at her death and, even more, that he had not been able to provide her with a better life in her final years.

When Booker's mother died, the family fell apart. His stepfather, Washington Ferguson, was unemployed and his twelve-year-old sister, Amanda, tried to fill her mother's role as housekeeper. Dinner was often no more than a can of tomatoes with some crackers. Clearly, there was no money to help Booker return to Hampton, so he turned to his old friend, Mrs. Viola Ruffner. She gave him a job so he could earn money to return to school in the fall.

In June 1875, Booker T. Washington graduated from Hampton Institute at the age of nineteen. Booker had always wanted to do something meaningful with his life, and he considered several careers, including being a lawyer, a minister, or a teacher. The black community was beset by injustices, and they needed good lawyers. However, Booker decided to be a teacher. He had a secondary-school diploma and a certificate qualifying him to teach.

Washington spent the summer of 1875 working as a waiter in a Connecticut hotel. When he was called upon to serve his first meal, he was so nervous he could not function. He fled the dining room and was demoted to being a busboy, cleaning up tables. But within a few days he mastered the art of waiting on tables and got his old job back.

The town of Malden had a school for whites and a separate one for blacks. Some local whites felt they paid too much in taxes to keep the white school going, and they were not willing to spend much for the black school in Tinkersville. The bureau said they "must provide for the white children first; they could not provide for both at once."[6] So the black school was held in a small black church with no heating.

The black directors of the Tinkersville school chose Booker T. Washington to be a teacher. He would be teaching at the same school he had attended as a child. But before he could collect his salary, he had to satisfy the white superintendent of schools in Kanewha County. All new teachers had to pass a tough examination. There is no

◆◆◆◆◆◆◆◆◆◆◆◆◆◆◆◆◆◆◆◆◆◆◆◆

Monthly Salaries for Teachers in Kanewha County in 1875

Whites		Blacks	
MEN	**WOMEN**	**MEN**	**WOMEN**
$41.10	$36.06	$31.50	$32.50

record of Washington's score on the test, but he was certified to teach all elementary school grades. As Washington started his teaching career, he described this day as "the beginning of one of the happiest periods of my life."[7]

Washington rented a small wooden house in Tinkersville with another teacher. Washington was very dedicated and not only taught the basics of reading and arithmetic, but also tried to improve the quality of the students' lives. He taught personal hygiene, including the proper way of brushing teeth, grooming hair, and caring for clothing. "I insisted that each pupil should come to school clean, should have his or her hands and face washed and hair combed," Washington wrote.[8]

Washington taught eighty to ninety students during the day, and almost a hundred more in night school. He also taught Sunday school at Zion Baptist Church and at Snow Hill, about three miles from Malden. Washington's work schedule was exhausting. He was the only teacher in Tinkersville. His day began at 8 A.M. and continued until 10 P.M. He was always on the alert for the brightest and best students, those who would qualify for Hampton Institute. He sent several boys and one girl, Fanny N. Smith, to Hampton. Smith was a bright young woman, and Washington was very fond of her.

Washington started a reading room for blacks in the local library and he formed debating clubs for his students. He tried to make his school a mini–Hampton Institute. He

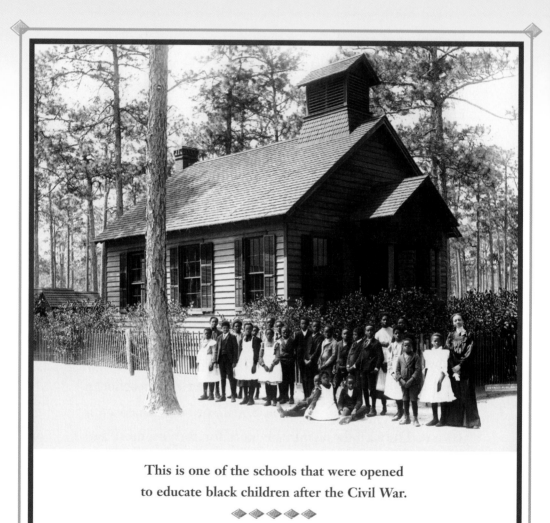

This is one of the schools that were opened
to educate black children after the Civil War.

even tried to duplicate the military drill. Since Washington could not afford rifles for his students, he marched them up the hill each morning with sticks on their shoulders in military formation.

When the school year ended at Tinkersville, there were elaborate ceremonies. The whole community was invited to take part. Mothers sewed new dresses for their girls, and boys got new jeans and jackets. All the students recited poems or speeches, or sang songs to the delight of their parents. Each child had a moment to shine.

Through Washington's efforts at Tinkersville school many children were given opportunities to succeed. Many became professionals, including lawyers and doctors. One graduate, Samuel E. Courtney, went on to Harvard Medical School and became a prominent Boston physician.

Though he took great satisfaction in teaching at Tinkersville, Booker T. Washington wanted something more. One of his pupils, W. T. McKinney, later recalled talking to Washington and noticing, "You always appeared to be looking for something in the distant future. There was always seen a future look in your eyes."[9]

In the fall of 1878, Booker T. Washington left Kanewha Valley to attend Wayland Seminary, a small Baptist Theological Seminary in Washington, D.C. Wayland was Washington's first contact with city living and higher education. Wayland was a training school for preachers and Washington said of his experience there, "I derived a great deal of benefit from the studies which I pursued."[10]

Washington was critical of black social life in Washington, D.C. He criticized the young black man who earned four dollars a week only to spend two dollars for a buggy ride on Sunday. He also disapproved of the young black women wearing the latest fashions.

Though still a very young man, Washington had formed the attitudes that would continue throughout his life. He favored practical education that imparted useful skills over intellectual study. He was offended by money wasted on unnecessary luxuries.

Over the spring of 1879, Booker T. Washington's life was about to take another major turn.

Chapter 4

The Road to Tuskegee

ooker T. Washington was invited by General Armstrong to deliver the graduation speech at Hampton Institute on May 22, 1879. Washington titled his address, "The Force That Wins" and he rehearsed it many times. In the address he told the students that success depended not only on education, but also on "wisdom and common sense, a heart bent on the right and a trust in God."[1] The speech was well received. Washington's former teacher at Hampton, Nathalie Lord, recalled years later, "I can see his manly figure, his strong, expressive face, and hear his voice, so powerful and earnest."[2]

Washington returned to Malden for a few weeks in the summer of 1879, uncertain about his future. He then received an invitation from General Armstrong to teach at Hampton Institute for $25 a month. The letter also invited

Washington to bring along a deserving student. At the time Armstrong made the offer, Hampton was undergoing changes in the racial makeup of its faculty. The previously all-white faculty was moving toward becoming partly black. In spite of this progress, black teachers like Washington would not have the same status as the white teachers. The black teachers would be called "graduates," while the white teachers were called "teachers."

When Washington arrived at Hampton, he taught classes and received training in advanced subjects. One of Washington's courses was at night for students who were very poor but had a deep thirst for knowledge. They worked eleven hours a day in the sawmill or laundry room at Hampton, and took classes at night. Washington said of these students, "I never taught pupils who gave me such genuine satisfaction."[3] The students showed so much desire to learn that Washington nicknamed them "The Plucky Class," praising their courage, spirit, and determination. Students who earned that nickname were awarded a certificate that officially declared them to be "a member of the plucky class."[4]

The student body at Hampton was entirely black for its first ten years except for one white student. In 1878 American Indian students were admitted. Washington was appointed housefather in the 1880–1881 school year. A housefather is responsible for guiding students and helping them with their problems while they reside at school.

Here, one of Hampton's American Indian students
talked to a class studying American history.

The first Indian students admitted to Hampton were federal prisoners of war captured during conflicts in the American West. The first group consisted of seventeen Kiowa and Cheyenne youths.

It was Booker T. Washington's task to teach the Indian youths the white man's way. The Indians hated having their long hair cut and not being allowed to wear blankets, as they had always done. The United States government gave Hampton strict instructions on how to treat the Indians. Their own religious and cultural traditions had to be driven out of them so they would better fit into white society. Washington found this troubling, but he went along with it. He commented, "No white American ever thinks that any other race is wholly civilized until he wears the white man's clothes, eats the white man's food, speaks the white man's language, and professes a white man's religion."[5]

Washington did his best to make the Indians conform to white standards. They had to walk in shoes, marching in step, and wear white man's clothing. The Indians called Washington "Mr. Booker T. Washington" and they obeyed him but did not bond with him. To the Indian boys he was forcing them into an unwanted way of life. Washington taught them such things as courtesy, handling silverware, and waiting to sit down at a table until all the women and girls are seated.

◆◆◆◆◆◆◆◆◆◆◆◆◆◆◆◆◆◆◆◆◆◆◆◆◆◆◆◆

Living Like White Men

After many wars between American Indians and white settlers, a new United States government policy was adopted in the 1880s. Called "detribalization," the goal was to break up Indian reservations and encourage the Indians to become farmers. Many Indian youths were sent to white boarding schools, where it was hoped they would abandon their own traditions and learn to live the white man's way.

While serving as housefather to the Indians, Washington was asked to take an ailing Indian student to the railway station to be returned to the reservation. Washington and the boy were riding on the Norfolk Ferry when supper was served. The pair walked together to the dining room and the Indian boy was immediately admitted, but Washington was stopped. He was told that he had to wait until everyone else in the dining room had eaten, because they could not be expected to share the dining room with a black man. Although the Indian boy had darker skin than Washington, the waiter made it clear that he considered the African American to be inferior.

In May 1881, General Armstrong received a letter from Tuskegee, Alabama, asking that he recommend a white teacher to come to Tuskegee to open a school similar to Hampton Institute. The white educational establishment at Tuskegee had learned from local black leaders of the good work being done at Hampton. They wanted someone like General Armstrong to educate the black youths of Tuskegee.

Tuskegee was a small town situated in the low Appalachian foothills. It had a population of two thousand people, about half black and half white. Tuskegee sat in the "black belt" of the South, a region so named because of its dark, naturally rich soil.

Not all the whites of Tuskegee wanted a black school in their town. But the majority of whites welcomed the idea of a school if only for the reason that it would provide jobs in a town sorely in need of another payroll. Once a rich cotton center, Tuskegee was now poverty stricken. Even the railroad passed by the town, building a station in Chehaw instead, a town five miles north.

Armstrong wrote back to Tuskegee that Washington, a black man, is "the best man we have ever had here," adding, "Is being colored an objection?" He recommended Washington, saying, "I know of no white man who could do better."[6] A week passed before the reply came from Tuskegee. "Booker T. Washington will suit us. Send him at once."[7]

Washington said goodbye to his friend Fanny Smith, who was still studying at Hampton, and he boarded a train for Alabama. He never had been in the Deep South before, and he did not know what to expect.

The initial idea for the black school in Tuskegee had come from two very different Tuskegee citizens who worked together to hatch the plan. One was George Lewis, a former slave who was now a leader in the black community in town. Lewis had never attended school himself, but he valued education and had taught himself to read and write. The other man, George W. Campbell, was a white former slaveholder, now a merchant banker.

> "I have learned that success is to be measured not so much by the position that one has reached in life as by the obstacles which he has overcome."[8]

Because they liked Republican president Abraham Lincoln, the blacks in the South, including those in Alabama, voted solidly Republican. Campbell, a Democrat, knew that Lewis had great influence in the black community. So Campbell made a deal with Lewis. If Lewis could persuade many black people to vote Democratic, then Campbell would help bring a black school to Tuskegee. The deal was made, and together these two men wrote the letter that brought Booker T. Washington to Tuskegee.

Booker T. Washington was expecting to take over leadership of an existing school in Tuskegee. When he arrived, he discovered that there was no school. There was not even a space set aside or plans to build a school. He did

These three ramshackle buildings were the only existing structures
on the plantation that would become Tuskegee Institute.

find a hundred-acre plantation south of town with a few
broken-down buildings. That was all. Washington and the
citizens of Tuskegee decided the farm would be a good
place to build the school. In the meantime, classes would
have to be held in temporary quarters. Those turned out
to be a shanty and the A.M.E. (African Methodist
Episcopalian) Zion Church in Tuskegee.

Chapter 5

Founding of Tuskegee and Family Life

efore school got started, Booker T. Washington wanted to learn as much as possible about the black people he would be serving. So in June 1881, he traveled all through Alabama to become familiar with the daily life of the people. Washington found large families living and sleeping in one room, eating cornbread and fat pork as their only diet. In a rundown cabin, a family of five had one fork to share, yet in this same cabin there was an expensive organ that the family was paying off in monthly installments. The people were easy prey for the traveling salesmen with persuasive sales pitches. Sixty-dollar sewing machines sat in the corners of shanties, though no one in the family could sew.

Washington concluded, "These people needed not only book learning, but knowledge on how to live."[1]

As Washington toured the countryside, he lived with the people he visited. He slept on the floor, as most of them did, and, like them, he bathed in nearby streams. After visiting the homes, Washington then looked at the local schools. There were few books for the students. Five students would commonly be reading from one book, two reading it, two peering over their shoulders, and one looking over the shoulders of all four.[2]

On July 4, 1881, twenty-five-year-old Booker T. Washington opened his school in Butler's Chapel of the A.M.E. Zion Church. The classes were held in a shanty adjoining the church. The building was shabby and inadequate, but Washington pledged there would be a real school building as soon as he could manage it.

Thirty students made up the first class at Tuskegee. Only students ages fifteen and up were accepted. Most of them were much older. They were poorly trained public school teachers hoping to improve their skills and advance to a higher teaching certificate so they could earn more money. A few of the teachers brought their teenaged students with them, and sometimes the youngsters knew more than their teachers.

The roof of the shanty was full of holes, and when it rained a student would stand beside Washington holding an umbrella over his head while he taught. At the boarding house where Washington lived, the roof leaked as well, and the landlady would shield her tenants with an umbrella as they ate their breakfast.

Some of the students at Washington's school had unusual knowledge, which Washington considered worthless at this time in their education. They knew French grammar and the geography of China, but lacked enough basic mathematics to figure out a grocery bill, or enough English to write a good letter.

By the end of the first month, the enrollment at Tuskegee School had grown to fifty students and Booker T. Washington was the only teacher. But after school had been under way for about six weeks, in August 1881, Washington was joined by another teacher, Olivia Davidson. The twenty-seven-year-old Davidson was from Ohio, where she had attended public schools. Like Washington, she was very devoted to educating black youth. As a teenager, she spent five years teaching children on Mississippi plantations. Then she entered Hampton Institute and graduated with honors. To become even more qualified to teach, Davidson enrolled at a teacher training institution, Framingham State Normal School in Massachusetts. A friend who knew her well, the Reverend R.C. Bedford, said that at Tuskegee she found "her field of labor for life. Everything tended to inspire her to this end."[3]

Olivia Davidson

When he was not teaching classes, Booker T. Washington spent nearly every waking hour trying to raise money to build a proper school. The farm he had decided on, known as the Bowen place, was for sale for $500. The owner told Washington that he could pay half up front and the balance at the end of the year. The treasurer at Hampton Institute lent Washington the money, and the deal was made.

Once a large home had stood on the Bowen place, but it burned to the ground. Now all that remained was a cabin, an old kitchen shed, a hen house, and a stable. Washington and his students went about fixing the old buildings into a school. The stable and hen house became classrooms, and the cabin and old kitchen were turned into housing.

Olivia Davidson was not only an enthusiastic and gifted teacher, but an eager fund raiser. She was as much on fire with zeal for the advancement of the students as Washington was. She held frequent suppers on the Bowen farm to raise money for the eventual building of the school. Davidson went door-to-door in Tuskegee, stopping at every house and asking black and white people alike for donations of cakes, pies, bread, and chicken to be used for the suppers or sold there. Hardly anyone turned her down.

The town of Tuskegee went all out to help Washington and Davidson. People donated dishes and eating utensils for the students. The local sawmill offered to donate all the lumber that would be needed in the school construction.

Washington got bids for the new building and learned it would cost $6,000 to complete the project. His friendship with General Armstrong at Hampton Institute put him in touch with whites who, like Armstrong, cared about the advancement of black people. Washington contacted wealthy white people in the North who were known to be sympathetic to the plight of former slaves and their children, and he asked for money. One of these benefactors was Alfred Haynes Porter, a businessman from Brooklyn, New York. He gave Washington the bulk of the money needed to build Tuskegee Institute.

One elderly black lady, leaning on a cane, donated all she had in the world—six eggs—saying she gladly gave it for the education of the "boys an' gals."[4]

In gratitude, Washington decided to name the building Porter Hall.

In the fall of 1881 and much of 1882, Washington and Davidson taught classes in the church school, sometimes at local public schools, and sometimes in the makeshift facilities of the farm. Every day after school, Washington marched the students to the farm to prepare the site for construction. Washington, wielding an axe, led the work

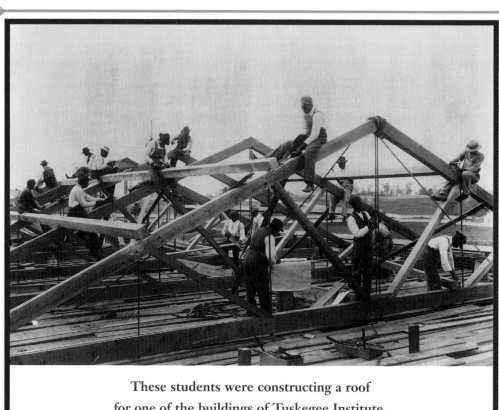

These students were constructing a roof
for one of the buildings of Tuskegee Institute.

crew in cutting down trees. They rapidly cleared an area in the forest, making twenty acres ready for construction.

By September 1881, there were sixty students living in the broken-down buildings of the Bowen farm and attending classes in town. Donations of maps, newspapers, and books came pouring in from surrounding towns and from the North. Many donations came from Hampton Institute. In preparation for building Porter Hall, the students made chairs and desks that consisted of planks nailed to the back of the seat in front. While the foundation was being dug, Washington and his students tilled the soil in other areas and planted many vegetables. Washington did not want his students living on pork fat and cornbread. They needed vegetables, too.

In March 1882, when the white teachers of Tuskegee met to select textbooks for the coming term, they invited Booker T. Washington to be on the committee. He was the first African American to ever serve on this committee.

When the school year ended, the Tuskegee Institute consisted of a half-built Porter Hall and a cluster of broken-down buildings. But Washington and Davidson held a picnic to celebrate the school's first year of operation. Black and white townspeople overflowed the grounds to hear students present songs and poetry readings.

In the summer of 1882, Washington and Davidson set out on separate trips to New England to raise more money. Davidson went to wealthy white neighborhoods asking for help for the poor black school down South. She spoke at churches on Sunday explaining the purpose of Tuskegee Institute with deep passion. Davidson was so exhausted at the end of each day that she was too tired to undress herself and would fall asleep on the couches of homes where she was staying, still fully clothed. Washington also contacted wealthy New Englanders. There was a spirit of sympathy for black people in New England and now the people realized that the freedmen depended on places like Tuskegee to make their way in the world. They were very receptive to the pleas of Davidson and Washington.

In June 1882, Fanny N. Smith graduated from Hampton Institute and returned to Malden. Booker T. Washington joined her there, and they were married on August 2, 1882, at Pastor Rice's Baptist Church in Tinkersville. The couple then traveled together to Tuskegee to begin their married life in a large rented house near the Tuskegee campus. The house not only served the Washingtons, but it also became a teacher's residence for the Tuskegee faculty, which had now grown to four teachers, including Davidson. By the end of the following year there would be ten teachers.

As Porter Hall was under construction, Washington frequently ran out of money. Once he owed a building material supplier $400 and he did not have one penny. On the final day the bill was due, $400 arrived from two wealthy Boston ladies who had been persuaded to help by Olivia Davidson. Later, these same women decided to donate $6,000 every year to Tuskegee.

When the frame structure was up, Porter Hall was three stories high. The basement would hold the kitchen, commissary (store selling food and supplies), dining room and laundry. The first floor held six classrooms, while the second floor held the chapel, reading room, and library. The third floor was used as a dormitory for the female students. Porter Hall looked like a large barn, but it was the largest building in town.

In the spring of 1883, Booker T. Washington embarked on a project that was to cause him great difficulty. He strongly believed in teaching industrial skills to students at Tuskegee. Since there was no brickyard in the town, and one was needed, he decided to lead his students in a brick-making venture. The clay soil in the northern part of Macon County was rich in kaolin, a fine white clay excellent for making bricks. Washington found a clay bank, and he and his students started digging. Washington had no knowledge of how to make bricks, nor did anyone else at Tuskegee.

Washington thought brickmaking was simple and expected to master it quickly. The work was hard and dirty, and some of the students complained, but Washington forged on. The first twenty-five thousand bricks Washington made were placed in the kiln they had built,

Turning Clay Into Bricks

◆◆◆◆◆◆◆◆◆◆

Bricks are made from clay. Clay is slippery and easily molded when wet, but hard and stony when dry. After a clay brick is cut from damp clay soil and molded, it is placed in a kiln (oven) and it changes chemically. The clay bricks turn red as they are burned or baked. Forever after, they remain hard and waterproof, making an excellent building material.

but the bricks did not bake properly and quickly returned to soft mush. Washington and his students had stood for hours in mud and cold water in the clay pits, and now they had nothing to show for their work.

Another batch of bricks was made. Using trial and error, Washington baked these, too, but they quickly fell apart. Finally, Washington hired an experienced bricklayer to guide him. On their fourth attempt, in a newly built kiln and under the direction of the bricklayer, Washington turned out a batch of first-class bricks. Brick-making quickly became a major industry at Tuskegee, with many students learning the skill. The finished bricks became the building blocks of Porter Hall.

By mid-October 1883, Porter Hall was still not completed, and Washington was tormented by financial woes. "I would roll and toss on my bed," he recalled later, "because of the anxiety and uncertainty."[5] Porter Hall was finally completed for the 1883–1884 school year. Washington taught rhetoric (the study of writing or

Tuskegee students learned how to make bricks
and then used them for building.

speaking), grammar, and composition. Davidson taught mathematics, astronomy, and botany. Other teachers taught natural sciences such as biology, bookkeeping, history, spelling, and geography. One hundred sixty-nine students were enrolled for the school year.

On June 6, 1883, the Washington's first child, Portia Marshall Washington, was born. She was the first baby born on the Tuskegee campus. In spite of Washington's hard work and frequent fund-raising trips, he took time to enjoy his family. He told friends his family was a "great comfort" to him.[6]

At the start of May 1884, Fanny Washington fell from a farm wagon, suffering internal injuries. She lingered for a few days before dying on Sunday, May 4, probably from complications from her injuries. She was buried on the Tuskegee campus. Washington wrote in tribute to her, "From the first, my wife most earnestly devoted her thoughts and time to the work of the school."[7]

Fanny Washington's mother, Celia Smith, came to help with the care of Portia, but soon the grieving husband turned to Olivia Davidson for comfort. Davidson had been his close friend since the founding of the school in 1881. On August 11, 1885, twenty-nine-year-old Booker T. Washington married thirty-one-year-old Olivia Davidson. The two worked side-by-side as school principals and as husband and wife. Olivia Washington was a genteel, graceful woman admired by the students at Tuskegee.

Washington and his family lived in this house on the Tuskegee campus.

Comfortable in his marriage, Washington took time to visit his brother and sister in Malden and to resume his fund-raising. He worked himself into exhaustion in the fall of 1885. All his life, Washington suffered from indigestion, which he self-medicated with papaya tablets. Olivia Washington persuaded him to take some time off to relax and recover his strength.

In 1886, Booker Taliferro Washington Jr. was born. His sister Portia called him "Brother," and that became his pet name. When Washington was away fund-raising, his wife wrote him loving letters telling him of the children's activities and closing with gentle advice,

> "Take care of yourself. *Keep your feet dry*. Kisses & love from the children & your loving
>
> Olivia."[8]

Although Olivia Washington dutifully cared for the children, taught at Tuskegee, and went on fund-raising trips herself, she was not strong. She suffered from weak spells, which the doctors could not diagnose. She may have been anemic (lacking in enough red blood cells) or even had tuberculosis (a serious lung disease common at the time). On February 8, 1889, after the birth of her second child, Ernest Davidson Washington, there was a fire in the Washington home. It was caused by a chimney defect. While Booker T. Washington was in the North raising money, his wife and children escaped the flames at four in the morning. The shock of the fire, along with exposure from standing out in the cold night, undermined Olivia Washington's already frail health. When her husband returned, he found her very ill. He took her to Massachusetts General Hospital in Boston for treatment. For three months, with her husband constantly at her side, Olivia Washington weakened. On May 9, 1889, she died.

At thirty-three-years-old, Booker T. Washington was again a widower, now with three children: six-year-old Portia, three-year-old Booker Jr., and baby Ernest. Olivia Washington's death devastated her husband emotionally and almost ruined him financially. For all the months of her illness, bills were piling up and he was neglecting his fund-raising. He had to borrow money to bring his wife's body back from Massachusetts to Tuskegee, where she was laid to rest beside Fanny Washington. The inscription on her tombstone read, "She lived to the truth."[9]

Booker T. Washington struggled to pick up the pieces and go on without the woman who had supported him for the past eight years, first as a valued colleague, then as a beloved wife and mother to his children.

Chapter 6

Washington's Way

When slavery ended after the Civil War, there was a brief effort to grant full equality to the former slaves. The 1875 Civil Rights Act forbade discrimination against black people. However, in reality, the black population of the South moved from slavery into the era of segregation. Schools, hospitals, libraries, parks, and most public accommodations were racially separated by the late 1880s. In 1883 the United States Supreme Court declared the Civil Rights Act unconstitutional, deciding that the federal government would not become involved in discrimination. Booker T. Washington was not unduly alarmed by this. He did not see government as a necessary partner in black progress. He believed the black race would advance by its own efforts and the good will of the whites who controlled government and wealth. Washington's message to his

Washington went through a difficult time after his wife's death.

people was to learn practical skills and improve themselves so white people would welcome them as competent workers.

Booker T. Washington's appearance changed dramatically after the death of his second wife. He shaved his mustache and gained considerable weight. He no longer looked boyish. A number of nursemaids were hired to care for his three motherless children. Olivia Washington's sister, Washington's brother, John, and his wife, Susie, came to Tuskegee to help with the children. Years earlier, when Washington had taught school at Tinkersville, he took a deep interest in an orphan boy, adopting him and naming him James Washington. Now James and his wife, Hattie, joined the extended family to help out.

In the spring of 1889, while visiting Fisk University in Nashville, Tennessee, to give a speech to the graduating class, Booker T. Washington met Margaret James Murray, a dedicated young teacher. They quickly became friends. Twenty-four-year-old Murray had been born in Macon, Mississippi. Her father died when she was seven and she was sent to live with the Sandlers, a white brother and sister, both teachers.[1] When Margaret was fourteen, her foster parents asked her if she would like to teach.[2] She said yes, and the next day she put on a long skirt, tied her hair in a bun, and began teaching in the same room where a day before she had been a student. Margaret found she liked teaching, but needed more education, so, at age nineteen she enrolled at Fisk University.

Washington was impressed with Murray's approach to education, which was similar to his own. They both believed young people needed a practical education that would prepare them for gainful employment. Washington hired Murray to teach English at Tuskegee. In 1890, she was appointed a principal at Tuskegee. Murray was a well-groomed, attractive woman with a good sense of humor. She liked Washington, but he seemed very reserved and difficult to know well. She wanted to tell him that she liked him, but she could not find the right words. She began calling him "My dear Mr. Washington," moving quickly to "My Dear Booker."[3]

Margaret Murray was fond of Washington's youngest child, Ernest, and she often cared for him. She also had a good relationship with Booker Jr., but eight-year-old Portia was cold toward her. Portia had accepted Olivia Davidson as her mother after the death of Fanny Washington, but she was not ready to accept another woman in her life. Right after Olivia Washington's death, the three children slept in their father's room. He spent a lot of time with them and this was especially meaningful to Portia. Portia resented her father's growing friendship with Murray. Portia felt Murray was taking her only remaining parent, her father, away from her.

In the fall of 1891, thirty-five-year-old Booker T. Washington proposed marriage to Margaret Murray. She hesitated to accept his offer right away because of the way

Washington and Margaret Murray, with his daughter, Portia, and sons Booker Jr. and Ernest Davidson.

Portia felt, but eventually she did agree. Murray married Washington on October 12, 1892, in Tuskegee.

During the 1890s, Booker T. Washington's life became entangled with that of Thomas A. Harris, a middle-aged black lawyer who had come to Tuskegee. The relationship between Harris and Washington was to become symbolic of the way Washington dealt with racial issues and how his critics felt about his behavior.

The whites of Tuskegee never had a problem with Booker T. Washington because he was respectful of their opinions and he never publicly criticized them. Thomas Harris was a different kind of black man. Born a slave, after the Civil War he became very active in politics. He was one of the freedmen who believed that with freedom should come equality. He was not willing, as Washington was, to wait patiently for the day when whites would voluntarily grant black people their civil rights. Harris attended Republican Party rallies and demanded equality

"A Fair Chance"

On May 26, 1892, Frederick Douglass, the best-known black leader of the time, delivered the graduation speech at Tuskegee Institute. Douglass, born into slavery, had become a famous orator against slavery and oppression. He urged the new graduates to use thrift and common sense. To the whites he threw out a challenge. "Give us a fair chance," he said, "but be sure you *do* give us a fair chance."[4]

Frederick Douglass

now. The white people of Tuskegee were alarmed. He seemed to be a dangerous troublemaker.

Harris had briefly practiced law in Birmingham. Now, in 1895, he opened a law office in Tuskegee. The very idea of a black lawyer in town was unwelcome to the white people. In June 1895, Harris invited a young white minister to spend several days in his home. One night, during a rainstorm, the minister was seen walking from church holding an umbrella as Harris's two daughters walked on either side of him. The sight of the two young black women walking so close to a white man enraged the white people.

A white mob formed the following day in front of the Harris home. Harris was told to leave town by 6 P.M. Harris refused and a lynch mob, complete with burning torches, formed. "There they are now, coming to kill me," Harris cried.[5]

Harris fled his home and ran into the yard of a white neighbor, John H. Alexander. Alexander tried to shove Harris off his property, but Harris would not leave. By now the lynch mob spotted Harris and began firing at him. Harris ducked and the bullet hit Alexander, who fell to the ground bleeding. The lynch mob fired again, this time hitting Harris and shattering his leg. While the white men in the mob were busy assisting the wounded Alexander, Harris was dragged away by his son. Thomas Harris, leaning on his son for support, arrived within the hour at the home of Booker T. Washington.

From that moment on, the story becomes clouded. It seemed that Washington had turned Harris and his son away. The local white newspaper highly praised Washington for this action, while local blacks condemned him. It looked to the blacks as if Washington had refused to aid a badly wounded black man just to appease the local whites. The truth of the matter came later and revealed the tightrope that Booker T. Washington walked on throughout his life. He always tried to keep the friendship of whites while helping his own people in the way he thought best.

On the night that Thomas Harris and his son came to Washington's door, Washington got out of bed and explained to the Harrises that if he took them into his home he would be risking the safety of all the students at Tuskegee. He would be exposing the whole school, he said, "to the fury of some drunken white men."[6]

What Washington did instead was to escort the Harrises to a safe place, and then get a doctor to come to treat Thomas Harris's leg wound there. Washington made sure Harris was cared for, but he did it all secretly. The story was verified later by Thomas Harris himself and the attending Doctor Dorsette. Three months later, Harris returned to Tuskegee to pick up his possessions before leaving the town.

"I remember all your kindness to me," said Thomas Harris to Booker T. Washington.[7]

Washington fed his chickens food grown in his own garden.

Booker T. Washington spent the early 1890s overseeing Tuskegee, raising funds, and in his rare free time, enjoying a peaceful life with his family. He enjoyed reading newspapers and nonfiction books, especially biographies. He read everything he could find on Abraham Lincoln, whom he described as "my patron saint."[8]

Washington read stories to his children and after the evening meal he took them for walks in the woods, teaching them the names of plants that grew there. Washington loved the sounds of different songbirds and he called the children's attention to the variety of chirps and trills. Washington even appreciated the sound of crickets. He loved to dig in his garden, planting seeds. He enjoyed raising animals and his favorite was the pig.[9]

In 1895, Washington was asked to give a speech in Atlanta before the Cotton States and International Exposition. This speech would change his life forever.

Chapter 7

"Cast Down Your Bucket Where You Are"

An audience of thousands of people, both blacks and whites, waited in Atlanta, Georgia, on September 18, 1895, to hear Booker T. Washington speak. As he entered the room, Washington later said he had noticed "considerable cheering" from the black section.[1] The title of his speech was "Cast Down Your Bucket Where You Are," and Washington quickly reminded whites that since black people were a third of the South's population, they could not be ignored. He urged whites to reach out to blacks because they had already contributed so much to the building of the South.[2] Washington promised his white audience that if they encouraged black educational and economic advancement, the result would be black people becoming

Washington knew how to keep the attention of his audiences.
Still, as time went on, his speeches drew mixed reactions.

"the most patient, faithful, law abiding, and unresentful people that the world has seen."[3]

Booker T. Washington then turned to the black people in the audience, urging them to cultivate friendly relations with their white neighbors and to train themselves to be successful in agriculture, mechanics, commerce, domestic service and the professions.

> "No race can prosper till it learns that there is as much dignity in tilling a field as in writing a poem."[4]

In one of the most significant parts of the speech, Washington said to whites, "In all things that are purely social we can be as separate as the fingers, yet one as the hand in all things essential to mutual progress."[5]

At the end of the speech, there was thunderous applause from the audience. People waved their handkerchiefs and canes and tossed their hats in the air. Many black people wept with joy or shouted agreement with Washington. The people of each race read into the speech what they wanted to hear. The blacks welcomed the appeal to whites to help blacks advance in the world. Whites saw in the speech an assurance that the social and political separation of the races could continue as long as black people were given some help to rise economically.

Cheered by the positive response to his speech from both races, Washington called the day after his speech, "the brightest, most hopeful day in the history of the Negro race."[6] Letters of praise poured into Tuskegee, hailing Washington as the new leader of the black race. Frederick Douglass, who had been recognized as the most prominent black leader in America, had died earlier in the year, on February 20, 1895. Now it seemed that Booker T. Washington was his successor as spokesman for black aspirations. Not everyone agreed with Washington's opinions, however. W.E.B. Du Bois, a young black Harvard graduate who was beginning to voice impatience with Washington's approach, believed Washington was a "compromiser between the South, the North, and the Negro."[7]

Almost immediately, after Washington's speech, there were voices of dissent from black communities in the North. George N. Smith, of the *Voice of Missions*, said that comparing Washington to Douglass was like "comparing a pygmy to a giant."[8] Smith and others saw Washington as a useful tool of the white community to help them maintain blacks in a second-class status. Many blacks had in fact boycotted the speech completely because they resented having to ride segregated buses and trains to get to Atlanta, and they refused to sit in an auditorium where blacks were segregated. They were in no mood to hear Washington's conciliatory tone. But among whites, praise for Washington reached new levels. He received numerous invitations to speak all over the country. He addressed black and white audiences, amusing his listeners with stories of Tuskegee and homespun folk tales from his childhood.[9]

As Booker T. Washington's fame grew, his wife, Margaret Washington, also became more active. She became president of the National Association of Colored Women's Clubs and she served as president of the Southern Federation of Colored Women's Clubs. She organized black women in Tuskegee and nearby communities in self-help programs.

In 1896, George Washington Carver, the genius in agricultural chemistry, joined the faculty at Tuskegee Institute. The orphan child of slave parents, Carver overcame poor health and inadequate early education to earn a B.A. and then master's degree in Agricultural and Mechanical Arts at Iowa State College. He taught agriculture at Tuskegee.

Booker T. Washington was invited to Harvard University to receive an honorary master of arts degree in June 1896. While beginning his address he felt uneasy at seeing the all-white audience, but he delivered his address.[10] Washington then went to Chicago to make the Chicago Peace Jubilee speech before an audience of sixteen thousand including President William McKinley. In that speech, Washington reminded the audience that when the United States called for help in the Spanish American War, blacks answered. He said that if a race was willing to

Margaret Murray Washington also became important
and influential in the African-American community.

Black Heroes

In 1898, the United States went to war against Spain to help Cuba, which was fighting for independence from Spain. At the time of the Spanish-American War, four African-American units were already part of the United States Army, and four more were organized for the war. Many blacks enlisted and saw action in the Cuban struggle. They served Theodore Roosevelt when he led the regiment nicknamed his Rough Riders up San Juan Hill in Cuba. The black soldiers served with honor and distinction.[11]

die for its country it deserved "the highest opportunity to live for its country."[12]

Washington invited President McKinley to come to Tuskegee. On December 18, 1898, the students passed in review before the president and other dignitaries. Each carried a stalk of sugar cane with a tuft of cotton on the end to demonstrate the importance of these crops. There was a colorful parade of floats, which were decorated wagons pulled by mules, horses, and oxen.

For several years, Walter Hines Page of Houghton Mifflin Publishing company had been urging Booker T. Washington to write his autobiography. Washington began gathering notes and dictating them to several young black writers. His notes were gathered into a rough draft.

Washington then did a great deal of rewriting until he was satisfied. His first book, *The Future of the American Negro*, a compilation of his articles and speeches, was published in December 1899. He continued to work on his autobiography.

Exhausted by his heavy schedule, Washington finally took a vacation in the summer of 1899. He and his wife sailed on the Red Star steamship *Friesland* from New York on May 10. Washington relaxed as he had not done in a long time. He slept fifteen hours a day on the ten-day passage. On the ship, the Washingtons received courteous treatment and suffered no racial discrimination from the ship's crew or its mostly white passengers. Everyone was friendly. When the ship reached Europe on August 5, the Washingtons toured England, France, and Holland. In England they met with the world-famous American writer Mark Twain and with Susan B. Anthony, who was campaigning for women's rights. In London, the Washingtons had tea with Queen Victoria.

When Washington returned to Tuskegee, he founded the National Negro Business League to increase opportunities for black businesspeople. Every American city with a large black population had a branch office. The meetings included testimonials from successful black businessmen.

In May 1900, Washington's first autobiography, *The Story of My Life*, was published. The following year the more popular *Up From Slavery* was published. The books were modest financial successes.

The Tuskegee Machine was the name given to an intricate set of black organizations, such as the National Negro Business League, dominated by Booker T. Washington and loyal to his philosophy. The machine lobbied Congress and wealthy white people for financial help for Tuskegee Institute. Booker T. Washington was a Republican, like most black people of that time. Washington became friendly with Republican President Theodore Roosevelt, who succeeded to the presidency after the assassination of President McKinley. Roosevelt told Washington he wanted to begin a new era of radical liberation for blacks in America. He asked Washington to be his adviser.

On the night of October 16, 1901, Booker T. Washington and President Roosevelt dined together at the White House. This angered many Southern whites, who saw it as a betrayal of Washington's promise to avoid black-white socializing. But many blacks took great pride in the fact that the president was according such honor to a black leader.

In spite of the Fifteenth Amendment to the Constitution which barred denying voting rights to anyone on the basis of race, the South managed through harassment of various kinds to prevent African Americans from registering to vote. Washington and his colleagues at

Theodore Roosevelt (holding a flower) and Booker T. Washington on a speakers' platform at Tuskegee in 1905.

Tuskegee got lifetime voting certification because he was on such good terms with the local whites. But ordinary black men, even successful businessmen and clergymen, could not vote. Washington secretly helped individual black would-be voters but he never spoke publicly on the issue.

Tuskegee Institute was becoming a magnet for students from Africa and Asia. At the time, white European governments ruled most of Africa as a colonial empire. These countries were trying to overthrow the political and cultural oppression of white rulers, and at Tuskegee they hoped to gain the skills and education to be successful. Washington quietly supported nationalist movements in Africa.

> Tuskegee was becoming a magnet for students from Africa and Asia.

Booker T. Washington not only strove to improve Tuskegee Institute, but he helped establish over one hundred small black schools in the South. He sponsored the Tuskegee Negro Conference to help black farmers. He and George Washington Carver developed Jesup Wagons, twelve-foot-long wagons that were agricultural schools on wheels to teach black farmers new techniques. Washington also promoted Negro Health Week, urging preventive medicine by fighting for clean water and sanitary methods of making milk, butter, and cheese.

Agricultural experts traveled around the country
helping farmers in rural areas.

Chapter 8

The Deepening Rift

B ooker T. Washington believed black schools like Tuskegee would develop strong and successful black men and women. He needed money for his work, and the wealthy white industrialists of the North had plenty. Washington moved his northern headquarters to New York, where he had access to these men. John D. Rockefeller of Standard Oil and Andrew Carnegie of United States Steel were admired by Washington as men with enormous wealth and power who donated to worthy causes. Washington flattered these men because he needed their support.

John D. Rockefeller also gave $10,000 a year to Tuskegee, and in 1902 John D. Rockefeller Jr. visited the school and built Rockefeller Hall there. Camera tycoon George Eastman read Washington's *Up From Slavery* and

Washington cultivated the friendship
of important men like Andrew Carnegie (circled).

Andrew Carnegie

Andrew Carnegie was born in Scotland in 1835. His family came to America when he was thirteen, and he went to work as a messenger at age fourteen. A railroad man took Andrew along as the rail and telegraph lines were set up during the Civil War. The boy picked up a lot of information, which he used to build his own businesses. He spent the last years of his life giving his millions away to worthy causes. Carnegie was the greatest single benefactor to Tuskegee Institute, donating $10,000 every year in addition to other gifts.

he was so impressed that he too contributed $10,000 a year to the school.

In a 1903 gathering in Madison Square Garden on behalf of the Tuskegee Institute, President Grover Cleveland gave an insensitive speech highlighting black shortcomings as a reason why they needed help. Washington listened solemnly, and then told the wealthy white audience that no matter what they believed black people lacked, Northern men of good will had to support black education. Carnegie made a large donation and called Washington, "One of the foremost of living men because his work is unique—the modern Moses who leads his race and lifts it through education."[1]

No wealthy man was more of a friend to Tuskegee than Julius Rosenberg, president of the department store Sears, Roebuck with its famous catalogue. He brought trainloads of rich friends to Tuskegee to show them around and inspire them to also become patrons of the school. He was very successful in adding new donors.

In 1903 conflict within Tuskegee Institute arose between the industrial and academic faculty. The industrial faculty stressed marketable skills like carpentry, brickmaking, and mechanics. The academic faculty searched out the most capable students to channel into college and one of the professions.

Many of the teachers in the industrial faculty were self-taught, and the academic faculty members, with their college degrees, felt superior to those without formal education. Some of the academic faculty had graduated from Fisk, Harvard, and Oberlin universities. Booker T. Washington hired twenty-four-year-old Roscoe Bruce, a Harvard graduate, as head of the academic faculty. His job was to bring peace between the two factions. Bruce required the academic faculty to visit the industrial department once a week, while the industrial faculty had their grammar checked by the academic faculty. Bruce believed this interaction would create harmony. Washington himself was more sympathetic to the industrial faculty because the vast majority of Tuskegee graduates would make their living with practical skills.

These students at Tuskegee were learning how to upholster furniture.

Washington held the faculty salaries at Tuskegee to a lower level than at most black schools. He wanted to be sure that the teachers at Tuskegee were so dedicated that they would be willing to work for less just for the opportunity to help needy students. As a result, Tuskegee teachers were overworked and underpaid.

As was the case at most schools of the time, there was a strict moral code at Tuskegee. No whisky, beer, or firearms were permitted. Card games were banned and a young man was not even permitted to escort a young woman home from chapel. One prominent faculty member, George Washington Carver, was even stricter than Booker T. Washington. Carver was offended when faculty called one another by their first names, and he demanded the practice be ended.[2]

Washington personally inspected the classrooms and dormitories to make sure all the rules were being followed. Pranks were severely punished. One year some seniors climbed the domed roof of one of the buildings to plant their class flag. They were dismissed from Tuskegee for the remainder of the year and had to wait until the following year to graduate.

The Washington children were growing up and choosing careers in the early 1900s. Portia Washington had never warmed to her stepmother and had spent several years living with friends. She returned to Tuskegee for her education and graduated in 1900. She taught music there for a year, then continued her education at Wellesley College before becoming a professional pianist in Berlin, Germany.

Booker Washington Jr. was attending school at Rockridge Hall in Wellesley, Massachusetts, while Ernest attended Oberlin Academy. A severe eye infection had left Ernest blind in one eye and impaired in the other. He was quite frail and he took a long vacation with his stepmother to recover his strength.

Booker's sons, Ernest Davidson, left, and Booker Jr.,
were almost grown when he adopted Laura in 1904.

Laura Murray, who was a niece of Margaret Washington's came to Tuskegee after the death of her parents. Laura was a small child, and the Washingtons adopted her. She became known as Laura Murray Washington. Laura was treated as a beloved child, especially cherished by Booker T. Washington.

Washington also kept in close contact with his sister, Amanda. She was in constant need of money and he never refused her. He arranged for her children to attend Tuskegee Institute.

Ever since his famous speech in Atlanta, Washington aroused the criticism of other black leaders unwilling to wait for equality to be given them through the goodwill of white people. In 1903, the criticism grew more intense. A younger generation of black leaders, born after the end of slavery, did not share Washington's philosophy. To survive and prosper, Washington had learned to be humble before the white power structure, but these young men wanted no part of that attitude.

Frustrated by Washington's acceptance of discrimination, the young men lashed out against Washington. Washington believed this group was a very small minority of the black community and, in truth, he continued to have the support of the majority of blacks.

A newspaper called *The Guardian* had been founded in 1901 by William Monroe Trotter, a black Bostonian and recent Harvard graduate. Its purpose was to fight "against discrimination based on color and denial of citizenship rights because of color."[3] Trotter denounced Booker T. Washington as subservient to whites and silent in the face of injustice. He condemned what he called "Washington's accommodationist policies and tactics."[4] A well-to-do real estate investor, Trotter organized a network of opposition to Washington's Tuskegee machine that spread to other black newspapers like the *Cleveland Gazette* and the *Chicago Conservator*. Washington tried to discredit Trotter, and Trotter tried to topple Washington as the leader of the black community. All of this came to a bitter and violent head on July 30, 1903.

The National Negro Business League invited Booker T. Washington to speak at the Columbus Avenue African Zion Church in Boston. Trotter planned to attend with his followers, intending to ask Washington embarrassing questions. He hoped he could expose Washington as a black leader who put the interests of white people first.

Expecting trouble, the Boston police sent eleven officers to the church. It was a hot night and the meeting opened with a prayer from a Washington supporter. When the first speaker referred favorably to Washington, the church filled with hisses. One Trotter supporter tried to approach the speaker's platform, but the police stopped him. Other Trotter people sprinkled cayenne pepper over the speaker's platform, causing widespread sneezing and coughing among the Washington supporters seated in the front rows. When Washington was introduced, chaos broke out. Some witnesses claimed the Trotterites hurled a stench bomb into the audience.[5] Shouts rained on Washington, making it impossible for him to speak. Fistfights broke out and one man was stabbed. Trotter leaped onto a chair and began reading a list of grievances against Washington. Few could hear his shrill voice in the din. Women began screaming and the billy-club wielding police charged in. Trotter was arrested and taken away. Finally Booker T. Washington was able to make his speech, but it was now apparent how deeply divided black leadership was.

Trotter got thirty days in jail for disturbing the peace and Washington approved because, he said, Trotter was "unrepentant."[6] Washington began compiling lists of his enemies in the black community, including W.E.B. Du Bois. Washington felt Du Bois had conspired with Trotter to disrupt his speech.

Actually, Du Bois was not involved in the church riot, though he sent a letter of sympathy to Trotter at his jailing and was later a house guest of the Trotters. W.E.B. Du Bois was indeed very opposed to Washington's philosophy. Du Bois unfavorably

> "Dr. Du Bois is very largely behind the mean and underhanded attacks that have been made upon me."[7]

W.E.B. Du Bois had strong disagreements
with Washington's beliefs.

reviewed Washington's book *Up From Slavery*, saying he relied too much on white friends. In his own book, *The Souls of Black Folk*, Du Bois accused Washington of asking black people to give up their dreams of equality, at least in the immediate future.[8] Du Bois claimed that Washington did not value "the privilege and duty of voting," and though Du Bois admitted he admired Washington's sincerity of

> Du Bois accused Washington of asking black people to give up their dreams of equality.

purpose, he said Washington represented an old attitude of adjustment and submission, which perpetuated the concept of the "inferiority of the Negro."[9]

Black leadership in America was now sharply divided between the supporters of Washington and of Du Bois. They were bitterly separated into warring camps. Washington used a list of Trotter supporters to harass with libel suits. Libel means defaming someone's character. Washington tried to put Trotter's newspaper out of business by setting up a rival newspaper and trying to steal the subscribers away.

In January 1904, Washington sponsored a conference of black leaders and white supporters at Carnegie Hall in New York. Washington believed it was still possible to pull Du Bois out of the Trotter camp, so he invited him. Du Bois came but commented on the "chilling presence" of Washington's white friends.[10] The rift was not healed.

Du Bois and the others started the Niagara Movement—
named after Niagara Falls—to fight for economic and
political rights for African Americans.

Chapter 9

Race Riots and the NAACP

O n June 5, 1905, W.E.B. Du Bois called a meeting on the Canadian side of Niagara Falls. The site was chosen because the hotels on the American side refused to rent rooms to the black attendees. The outcome of the meeting was the "Negro Declaration of Independence," which demanded full rights for blacks, abolition of racial discrimination, and the protection of all rights and liberties in the United States. The meeting came to be called the "Niagara Movement," and it soon was obvious that the rivalry between the supporters of Booker T. Washington and the more militant black leaders would continue.

In the years between 1898 and 1923, deadly race riots ravaged many American cities. They were especially violent in the early 1900s. Two serious incidents occurred in 1906 which exposed the reality of racial division in America.

The first battalion of the 25th Infantry regiment was transferred to Fort Brown, just outside Brownsville, Texas, during the summer of 1906. Except for its officers, it was an all-black unit. The soldiers were veterans of the Spanish-American War of 1898 and had an excellent record. However, the white people of Brownsville did not want a black regiment at Fort Brown. They feared the black soldiers might unite with the already large Mexican-American population, making the whites a minority.

On the morning of August 14, a fight broke out near Fort Brown. Shots were fired; a white bartender was killed and a policeman was wounded. The details of the incident were unclear. Some whites blamed black soldiers for the violence, claiming to have seen them firing off their guns. Based on this accusation, twelve members of the black regiment were arrested. However, no sound evidence could be gathered against the soldiers, and the charges were dropped. The United States War Department then sent investigators. All the soldiers in the regiment were assembled. Those who had participated in the violence were told to come forward and confess. No black soldier did so. All protested their innocence. Because none of the black soldiers admitted guilt, or implicated their brother soldiers, the entire battalion was charged with insubordination. The twelve soldiers originally charged were discharged "without honor," as were all the other 155 black soldiers.[1]

Booker T. Washington appealed directly to President Theodore Roosevelt not to sign the discharges. But the president ignored him. All the black soldiers were removed from service, losing their back pay and all pensions due them. It was an obvious injustice, since the white commanding officer of the unit vouched for all the men, saying they were in their barracks when the shooting took place. Many of the men were longtime soldiers, close to retirement and depending on their pensions for their old age. Six of the men had already won the Medal of Honor.

When President Roosevelt refused Washington's plea for justice, Washington accepted the bitter pill as he had accepted so many other slights. He thought if he argued further with Roosevelt he would lose access to the president, something he considered important in his agenda of helping black people advance. But many blacks who had believed President Roosevelt was a friend to their race felt betrayed by the harsh actions at Brownsville. Some also resented Washington for not showing righteous anger. It seemed to them that Washington would not lose his temper with powerful white people, and this dismayed them.

The following month, in September 1906, another violent racial riot took place, this time in Atlanta, Georgia. For months, racial hatred had been stirred up by a white effort to stop blacks from voting. The Atlanta press began a campaign of emphasizing black crime in the city by giving enormous publicity to any incident of black crimes

◆◆◆◆◆◆◆◆◆◆◆◆◆◆◆◆◆◆◆◆◆◆◆◆◆◆

Justice at Last

Convinced that the people of Brownsville had framed the black soldiers because they feared black men in uniform, the United States government finally righted the wrong in 1972, sixty-six years after the fact. President Richard Nixon signed a bill granting all the 167 discharged soldiers of the 25th Regiment "honorable discharges." Only one soldier was still alive, and he received $25,000 in compensation.

against whites. The newspapers gave the impression that white women were being victimized by black men all over the city.[2] Enraged white mobs descended on the black business district of Atlanta, dragging blacks from streetcars, saloons, and restaurants and beating them. The violence continued for four days, causing the deaths of ten blacks and two whites. Black homes and businesses were burned and hundreds were injured and forced to flee the city.

The twin disasters of Brownsville and Atlanta showed serious flaws in Booker T. Washington's philosophy that accommodation with the whites would lead to racial harmony. In August 1908, another race riot tore through Springfield, Illinois, where Abraham Lincoln had lived. A white mob beat black people at random and lynched two black men. Stunned by the violence, some prominent black leaders joined with sympathetic white people in New York City to form the National Association for the Advancement of Colored People (NAACP). Many of the principles of the NAACP came from the Negro Declaration of Independence first created by the Niagara Movement.

In the words of W.E.B. Du Bois, the task of the NAACP would be to deal with "the problem of the Twentieth Century—the problem of the color line."[3]

Booker T. Washington was angered and saddened by the racial violence, but he still would not publicly condemn the behavior of white men. The Du Bois followers refused to take such a conciliatory attitude. Oswald G. Villard, a journalist and one of the men behind the NAACP, invited Washington to the founding meeting of the NAACP, but many others in the group bitterly opposed Washington's even coming. Washington knew he was not welcome at the meeting, but he sent a colleague to see what was going on. Washington believed the NAACP would be used to discredit him and the Tuskegee Movement.

As Washington confronted new challenges from his critics, his children were starting families of their own. Portia Washington was married in 1907 to Sidney Pittman, an architect. Booker Washington Jr. married Nettie Hancock and was launching a business career. Ernest Washington married Edith Merriweather and

Washington's philosophy of accommodation with whites was not leading to racial harmony.

became a public relations officer for the Tuskegee Institute.

In 1909 Republican William Howard Taft became president. Booker T. Washington did not have the close relationship with Taft that he had with Roosevelt, but Washington still wielded some influence.

In 1910 Booker T. Washington's relationship with the NAACP became as bitter as he had feared it would. The two factions, Washington's followers and the members of the NAACP, were fighting for the hearts and minds of the black community. Washington blamed the rift on jealous men in the NAACP who resented his great success at Tuskegee. In an open letter to Booker T. Washington from Du Bois and thirty-one other prominent black leaders, Washington was denounced for saying, while on a trip to Europe, that race relations in the United States were improving.

In 1911 an ugly personal incident shook Booker T. Washington to his foundations. He arrived in New York to give speeches to black and white churches. At 9 P.M. on Sunday, March 19, he had finished his last speech. Heading to a friend's home, he became momentarily lost. While seeking information at an apartment building, he was suddenly attacked by a white man who punched him in the side of his head. Washington ran from the attacker, only to catch his foot on a trolley track and fall. His clothing torn and dirty, blood streaming from his head,

Washington staggered to his feet as a policeman approached. The white man who had attacked Washington accused Washington of being a burglar. The officer arrested Washington and took him to the police station, at first refusing to believe that he was Booker T. Washington. When Washington finally convinced the police of his identity and told his story, the white man, Henry Ulrich, was arrested for felonious assault. Washington was taken to nearby Flower Hospital, where sixteen stitches were taken to close his wound.

Things were never again quite the same for Booker T. Washington. In a personal and painful way, he learned what it was like to be an ordinary black man in a white world. If a man as prominent as he was could be so brutally attacked, then arrested on a lie, then what must life be like for the average black man without celebrity to shield the blows of injustice? Washington discovered that merely having black skin automatically made him a potential criminal in the eyes of white people. In a final sad blow, the white attacker was found innocent of all charges.

During the 1912 presidential election, Booker T. Washington remained loyal to the Republican Party and supported William Howard Taft even though he felt Taft was not receptive to most of his advice. The NAACP and William Trotter however turned to the Democratic candidate, Woodrow Wilson. Wilson pledged he would work for justice for all people.

When Wilson was elected president it gave Washington small comfort to know how right he had been in his choice. Wilson was no friend to black people and, in fact, fired many black office holders.[5] Worse yet, Wilson enforced tough segregation laws throughout the federal govern-

> "The colored people may count on me for absolute fair dealing."[4]
>
> —Woodrow Wilson

ment. Washington wrote angry, complaining letters to the president, but Wilson never responded. "I fear that the president's high sounding phrases regarding justice do not include the Negro," Washington lamented.[6]

In a diligent letter writing campaign, Booker T. Washington did gain a victory for blacks with the defeat in the House of Representatives of the African Exclusion Bill. This bill would have barred all African immigration even from the West Indies. The bill passed the Senate but failed in the House largely through the efforts of Washington and his friends.

Now aging rapidly, Booker T. Washington faced his final years beset by divisions in the black community.

Chapter 10

Death and Legacy

I n his last years, Booker T. Washington dealt with the same issues the NAACP was working on, but the methods used were very different. The NAACP established a northern base to challenge racial injustice through legal action. Behind the scenes, Booker T. Washington was using his personal funds and influence in legal test cases that accomplished many of the same objectives. In an article published in *Century Magazine* in 1912, Washington concluded that black people were not getting a fair chance, that they received unequal education, unfair treatment in the legal justice system and they were denied access to public facilities and the right to vote. Washington clearly recognized the problem, but it would fall to younger black leaders to find the solution.

Margaret Washington wrote in another article that the future advancement of blacks was in the hands of black women. "The revolution has begun, regeneration has set in, and these women who have gone through trials and tribulations are going to take their stand."[1]

Booker T. Washington launched a campaign to improve streetcar facilities for black riders through a program called Railroad Days. He clung to his

> Washington faced his final years beset by divisions in the black community.

philosophy that white men of goodwill would respond positively if they understood the problem. So on specific days, black riders went in groups to the railroad authorities to tell them that the cars were poorly ventilated, unlighted and dirty. The authorities listened politely but did nothing to improve the streetcars used primarily by black riders.

Washington was more successful when he dealt with residential segregation in Tuskegee. The town of Tuskegee had two black residential areas, one around the institute and another on the far side of town. The Tuskegee whites decided to make sure that even in rural areas of town, segregation by race would continue. They sponsored a law that the majority of landowners in every area of town had to approve the sale of a lot or house to persons of another race. Washington wrote an editorial that such a law could only inspire hatred between the races and was unnecessary. Moved by his arguments, the white people of Tuskegee did not pass the law.

Washington then moved to attack racial segregation in other parts of the country. He called such segregation "wholly unconstitutional."[2] In an article on the subject, Washington called residential segregation laws "unjust" and "unnecessary," and sure to widen the breach between the races.[3] Washington urged blacks to go all the way to the Supreme Court of the United States to fight residential segregation, but aside from a few newspaper articles, he campaigned mostly through private letters. His NAACP critics, therefore, again accused him of doing very little to advance black civil rights.

When Washington learned that Birmingham, Alabama, was considering laws making it illegal for blacks to buy homes in white neighborhoods, he again chose the nonconfrontational approach. He wrote privately to the Birmingham Board of Commissioners, saying the law was unnecessary because blacks did not really want to live in white neighborhoods. "It is unusual to hear of a colored man attempting to live where he is surrounded by white people or where he is not welcome," Washington wrote.[4] Washington's strategy stopped the Birmingham ordinance, but it did not solve the nationwide reality that black people were being barred from white neighborhoods throughout the United States.

At the urging of his family and friends, Booker T. Washington tried to take more time for rest and recreation. He took vacations at a fishing camp at Coden on the

Fishing helped Washington unwind from the pressures of his life.

west side of Mobile Bay. A breeze off the water kept the camp insect free and cool even on the hottest summer days. Washington enjoyed his time at the fishing camp.

Washington's bouts with ill health continued, and he suffered frequently from indigestion and fatigue. He spent some time at Battle Creek Sanitarium in Michigan and although the stay temporarily relieved his symptoms, his

FRED R. MOORE   DR. BOOKER T. WASHINGTON   J. C. NAPIER
       DR. A. B. JACKSON   DR. S. E. COURTNEY

The last photo of Washington, center front,
was taken at a Boston meeting of the National Negro
Business League in 1915 and published in the newspaper.

overall health continued to decline. Washington was aware of his frail health and he made out a will naming his wife as executor. He left his three children equal shares of his book royalties as well as proceeds from a life insurance policy. He left small amounts to other members of the family, including his brother, John. Washington's sister, Amanda Johnson, died of a stroke in 1915.

In August 1915, at a Boston meeting of the Negro Business League, Washington was obviously ill and nervous. He made a final fishing trip to Coden to revive his stamina. He planned to have a complete physical examination at the Mayo brothers clinic in Rochester, Minnesota, but he kept postponing it because his duties at Tuskegee Institute always came first.

On October 17, 1915, Washington gave the evening talk to the Tuskegee students in the chapel. Then he spoke at the national conference of Congregational churches in New York on October 25, though his blood pressure was high and he was suffering from kidney trouble. Two of Washington's closest friends, Seth Low and William G. Wilcox, insisted he go to Dr. W. A. Bastedo's office for a diagnosis of his worsening condition. Dr. Bastedo said Washington was suffering from Bright's disease (a kidney disease) and his life "was only a question of days."[5] Washington's friends then took him to Rockefeller Institute for Medical Research, where Dr. Rufus Cole gave the same diagnosis. However, in an effort to save

Washington's life, he was hurried to St. Luke's Hospital. Based on a doctor's report from St. Luke's, the New York *Tribune* reported that Washington was "completely worn out" and suffering from hardening of the arteries.[6] Washington was told he had little time left. In spite of his dire condition, Washington insisted on returning to Tuskegee. "I was born in the South, have lived all my life in the South, and expect to die and be buried in the South," he said.[7]

Margaret Washington helped her husband rise from his bed and get dressed. Leaning on her, he made his way to the street, refusing a wheelchair. Walking unsteadily, Washington reached the railroad station, where he boarded a train at 4 P.M. Friday afternoon. The train reached Tuskegee on Saturday at midnight. An ambulance would take him home. Washington reached his bedroom alive, but at 4:40 Sunday morning, November 14, 1915, Booker T. Washington died, surrounded by his family.

Letters of condolence poured into Tuskegee upon word of Washington's death. The body lay in state at Tuskegee chapel the day before the funeral. Three days after his death, Washington was buried. One of the largest crowds ever seen in Tuskegee came. They arrived by Pullman trains, automobiles, carriages, ox carts, or on foot. Black and white dignitaries and about eight thousand ordinary people came to pay their respects. Tuskegee graduate Isaac Fisher described the funeral service: "No labored

AFRO-AMERICAN MONUMENT.

In 1897 an artist put together Afro-American Monument. He wanted to show African-American history from the beginnings of slavery to the push for freedom, justice, and equality, spurred on by leaders like Booker T. Washington.

"One of the most useful citizens of our land has gone."[9]
—Theodore Roosevelt.

eulogies; no boastings of his great work; no gorgeous trappings of horses. . . . Just a simple, impressive . . . service."[8]

Washington was buried in the little cemetery on the Tuskegee campus. His gravestone carried only the date of his birth and death, but a granite boulder had been used.

Portia Washington Pittman devoted much of her life to overseeing the establishment of the Booker T. Washington Foundation to provide academic scholarships to worthy black students.[10]

In 1931, a bronze and granite monument in honor of Booker T. Washington was erected at Tuskegee Institute. Numerous United States stamps have honored him and, on March 29, 1956, noting the one hundredth anniversary of Washington's birth, President Dwight D. Eisenhower said Washington's "achievements as an educator and a leader in the betterment of human living are an inspiration to men and women of every race and an enduring memorial to his great gifts of mind and heart and character."[11]

Booker T. Washington gave his life to advance the educational opportunities for thousands of young black people. He labored in a humble, self-sacrificing way, demanding of himself extraordinary effort and devotion to his noble cause. When new black leaders arose to rightly

In this famous statue on the Tuskegee campus, Washington
is "lifting the veil of ignorance from his people."

demand a faster pace in the struggle for equality, Washington was hurt and bewildered. He was a creature of his time, a slave child who courageously built Tuskegee Institute from a shanty with thirty students to an impressive institution that has educated thousands. In 1915 Tuskegee had an enrollment of two thousand students with two hundred teachers and $2 million in the bank. Washington's legacy is in the successful lives of all those young people he rescued from hopelessness and ignorance.

Chronology

1856—Booker Taliferro is born near Hale's Ford, Virginia.

1865—Freed from slavery by the Emancipation Proclamation. Takes the name Booker T. Washington.

1872—Enrolls at Hampton Institute in Virginia.

1875—Graduates from Hampton Institute. Becomes a teacher in Malden, West Virginia.

1879—Becomes a teacher at Hampton Institute.

1881—Opens Tuskegee Normal School in Tuskegee, Alabama, July 4.

1882—Marries Fanny N. Smith in August.

1883—First child, Portia Marshall Washington, is born June 6.

1884—Fanny Washington dies May 4.

1885—Marries Olivia Davidson August 11.

1886—Second child, Booker T. Washington Jr., is born.

1889—Third child, Ernest Davidson Washington, is born. Olivia Washington dies.

1892—Marries Margaret Murray October 12.

1895—With "Cast Down Your Bucket Where You Are" speech in Atlanta, gains national fame.

1896—Receives honorary master of arts degree from Harvard.

1899—First book, *The Future of the American Negro,* published.

1900—Autobiography *The Story of My Life* published.

1901—Autobiography *Up From Slavery* published. Dines at the White House with President Theodore Roosevelt.

1903—Has speech interrupted in Boston by violent supporters of William Trotter.

1911—Suffers violent attack at the hands of Henry Albert Ulrich in New York.

1915—Dies in Tuskegee, Alabama, on November 14.

Chapter Notes

Chapter 1. Boy on Fire

1. Booker T. Washington, *Up From Slavery*, public domain text (originally published 1901), Chapter 3. <http://www.africanamericans.com/UpFromSlavery3.htm> (December 2, 2005).
2. Ibid.
3. Ibid.
4. Ibid.
5. Louis R. Harlan, *Booker T. Washington: The Making of a Black Leader 1856–1901* (New York: Oxford University Press, 1972), p. 55.
6. Washington, *Up From Slavery*, Chapter 3.
7. Ibid.
8. Harlan, *The Making of a Black Leader*, p. 55.
9. Washington, *Up From Slavery*, Chapter 3.

Chapter 2. Childhood

1. Louis R. Harlan, ed., *The Booker T. Washington Papers*, Vol. II (Chicago: University of Illinois Press, 2000), p. xxv.
2. Louis R. Harlan, *Booker T. Washington: The Making of a Black Leader 1856–1901* (New York: Oxford University Press, 1972), p. 3.
3. Ibid., p. 14.
4. Booker T. Washington, "Christmas Day in Old Virginia," *Suburban Life*, December 21, 1907, pp. 336–337.
5. Booker T. Washington, *Up From Slavery*, public domain text (originally published 1901), Chapter 1. <http://www.africanamericans.com/UpFrom Slavery1.htm> (December 2, 2005).

6. Booker T. Washington, "Early Life and Struggle for an Education," *Howard's American Magazine*, November 4, 1899, pp. 3–6.

7. Washington, *Up From Slavery*, Chapter 2. <http://www.africanamericans.com/UpFromSlavery2.htm> (December 2, 2005).

8. Booker T. Washington, "Chapters From My Experience," in Herbert Aptheker, ed., *Documentary History of the Negro People*, Vol. 3 (New York: Citadel Press, 1993), p. 3.

9. Washington, *Up From Slavery*, Chapter 3. <http://www.africanamericans.com/UpFrom Slavery3.htm> (December 2, 2005).

10. Ibid.

11. Ibid.

12. Harlan, *Black Leader*, p. 45.

Chapter 3. From Student to Teacher

1. Booker T. Washington, *Up From Slavery*, public domain text (originally published 1901), Chapter 3. <http://www.africanamericans.com/UpFromSlavery3.htm> (December 2, 2005).

2. Louis R. Harlan, *Booker T. Washington: The Making of a Black Leader 1856–1901* (New York: Oxford University Press, 1972), p. 56.

3. Booker T. Washington, *Up From Slavery*, Chapter 4. <http://www.africanamericans.com/UpFromSlavery4.htm> (December 2, 2005).

4. Ibid.

5. Ibid.

6. Louis Harlan, ed., *The Booker T. Washington Papers*, Vol. II (Chicago: University of Illinois Press, 2000), p. 15.

7. Washington, *Up From Slavery*, Chapter 4.

8. Harlan, *The Booker T. Washington Papers*, Vol. I, p. 24.

9. Harlan, *Black Leader*, p. 91.

10. Washington, *Up From Slavery*, Chapter 5. <http://www.africanamericans.com/UpFromSlavery5.htm> (December 2, 2005).

Chapter 4. The Road to Tuskegee

1. Louis Harlan, *Booker T. Washington: The Making of a Black Leader 1856–1901* (New York: Oxford University Press, 1972), p. 100.

2. Ibid., pp. 99–100.

3. Booker T. Washington, *Up From Slavery*, public domain text (originally published 1901), Chapter 6. <http://www.africanamericans.com/UpFromSlavery6.htm> (December 2, 2005).

4. Ibid.

5. Ibid.

6. Harlan, p. 110.

7. Ibid.

8. Washington, *Up From Slavery*, Chapter 2. <http://www.africanamericans.com/UpFromSlavery2.htm> (December 2, 2005).

Chapter 5. Founding of Tuskegee and Family Life

1. "Dr. Booker T. Washington, Negro Leader, Dead," *New York Times*, November 15, 1915, p. 1.

2. Booker T. Washington, *Up From Slavery*, public domain text (originally published 1901), Chapter 8. <http://www.africanamericans.com/UpFromSlavery8.htm> (December 2, 2005).

3. Louis Harlan, ed., *Booker T. Washington Papers*, Vol. I (Chicago: University of Illinois Press, 2000), p. 54.

4. Washington, *Up From Slavery*, Chapter 8.

5. Louis Harlan, *Booker T. Washington: The Making of a Black Leader 1856–1901* (New York: Oxford University Press, 1972), p. 139.

6. Ibid., p. 146.

7. Washington, *Up From Slavery*, Chapter 9. <http://www.africanamericans.com/UpFromSlavery9.htm> (December 2, 2005).

8. Louis Harlan, ed., *Booker T. Washington Papers*, Vol. 2 (Chicago: University of Illinois Press, 2000), p. 424.

9. Ibid., p. 531.

Chapter 6. Washington's Way

1. Louis Harlan, ed., *Booker T. Washington Papers*, Vol. 2 (Chicago: University of Illinois Press, 2000), p. 515.

2. Louis Harlan, *Booker T. Washington: The Making of a Black Leader 1856–1901* (New York: Oxford University Press, 1972), p. 181.

3. Ibid., p. 183.

4. William S. McFeely, *Frederick Douglass* (New York: W.W. Norton and Company, 1991), p. 363.

5. Harlan, *Black Leader*, p. 172.

6. Ibid. p. 174

7. Ibid.

8. Booker T. Washington, *Up From Slavery*, Chapter 15. <http://www.africanamericans.com/UpFromSlavery15.htm> (December 2, 2005).

9. Ibid.

Chapter 7. "Cast Down Your Bucket Where You Are"

1. Booker T. Washington, *Up From Slavery*, public domain text (originally published 1901), Chapter 14. <http://www.africanamericans.com/UpFromSlavery14.htm> (December 2, 2005).

2. Booker T. Washington, "'Cast Down Your Bucket Where You Are': Booker T. Washington's Atlanta Compromise Speech." <http://historymatters.gmu.edu/d/88/> (December 1, 2005).

3. Booker T. Washington (1856–1915): Speech at the Atlanta Exposition, 1895. <http://www.fordham.edu/halsall/mod/1895washington-atlanta.html> (June 30, 2004).

4. Ibid.

5. Ibid.

6. Louis R. Harlan, *Booker T. Washington: The Making of a Black Leader 1856–1901* (New York: Oxford University Press 1972), p. 222.

7. W.E.B. Du Bois, *The Souls of Black Folk* (New York: Alfred A. Knopf, 1993; first published in 1903), p. 44.

8. Harlan, p. 226.

9. Louis R. Harlan, ed., *The Booker T. Washington Papers*, Vol. 4 (Chicago: University of Illinois Press, 2000), p. xxi.

10. Harlan, *Black Leader*, p. 236.

11. Rayford W. Logan and Irving S. Cohen, *The American Negro* (New York: Houghton Mifflin, 1970), pp. 150–151.

12. Harlan, p. 237.

Chapter 8. The Deepening Rift

1. Louis A. Harlan, *Booker T. Washington: The Wizard of Tuskegee, 1901–1915* (New York: Oxford University Press, 1983), p. 135.

2. Ibid., p. 156.

3. Peter F. Stevens, "The Activist of Sawyer Avenue: William Monroe Trotter," *Dorchester Reporter*, February 21, 2002, p. 1.

4. Ibid.

5. Ibid.

6. Ibid.

7. Harlan, p. 50.

8. W.E.B. Du Bois, *The Souls of Black Folk* (New York: Alfred Knopf, 1993; first published in 1903), p. 45.

9. Ibid.

10. Harlan, p. 71.

Chapter 9. Race Riots and the NAACP

1. "Race Relations Under Theodore Roosevelt," <http://www.u-s-history.com/pages/h.943.html> (July 2, 2004).

2. Robert A. Gibson, "The Negro Holocaust: Lynching and Race Riots in the United States, 1880–1950" (New Haven: Yale-New Haven Teachers Institute, Vol. II, 1979), p. 6.

3. Louis R. Harlan, *Booker T. Washington: The Wizard of Tuskegee, 1901–1915* (New York: Oxford University Press, 1983), p. 360.

4. Peter Stevens, "The Activist of Sawyer Avenue: William Monroe Trotter," *Dorchester Reporter*, February 21, 2002, p. 5.

5. Louis Harlan, ed., *The Booker T. Washington Papers*, Vol. 12 (Chicago: University of Illinois Press, 2002), p. xvii.

6. Harlan, *Wizard*, p. 358.

Chapter 10. Death and Legacy

1. Mrs. Booker T. Washington, "Are We Making Good?" *The Independent*, October 4, 1915, p. 22.

2. Louis Harlan, *Booker T. Washington: The Wizard of Tuskegee, 1901–1915* (New York: Oxford University Press, 1983), p. 426.

3. Booker T. Washington, "My View of Segregation Laws," *New Republic*, December 4, 1915, pp. 113–114.

4. Ibid.

CHAPTER NOTES

5. "Learned His Doom Here," Booker T. Washington National Monument. <http://www.nps.gov/bowa/ edprogram11/btwobit.html> (July 2, 2004).

6. Harlan, p. 451.

7. "Dr. Booker T. Washington, Negro Leader, Dead," *New York Times*, November 15, 1915, p. 1.

8. Harlan, p. 456.

9. "Col. Roosevelt Grieved," Booker T. Washington National Monument. <http://www.nps.gov/bowa/ edprogram11/btwobit.html> (July 2, 2004).

10. "Portia Washington Pittman was committed like her Dad!," *The African American Registry*, <http://www. aaregistry.com/african_american_history/1701/Portia_Wash ington_Pittman_was_committed_like_her_dad> (July 10, 2004).

11. Booker T. Washington, "Posthumous Honors," *Up From Slavery* (New York: Doubleday and Company, Inc., 1963), p. 232.

Further Reading

Altman, Susan. *Extraordinary African Americans: From Colonial to Contemporary Times*. New York: Chelsea House, 2001.

Garrison, Mary. *Slaves Who Dared: The Stories of Ten African American Heroes*. Shippensburg, Pa.: White Mane Kids, 2002.

Roberts, Jack L. *Booker T. Washington: Educator and Leader*. Brookfield, Conn.: Millbrook Press, 1995.

Schroeder, Alan, with additional text by Anne Beier. *Booker T. Washington: Educator and Racial Spokesman*. New York: Chelsea House, 2005.

Swain, Gwenyth. *A Hunger for Learning: A Story about Booker T. Washington*. Minneapolis, Minn.: Millbrook Press, 2006.

Troy, Don. *Booker T. Washington*. Chanhassen, Minn.: Child's World, 1999.

Washington, Booker T. *Up From Slavery*. New York: New American Library, 2002. (New edition).

Internet Addresses

Booker T. Washington Papers: biography, photographs, and writings.
    <http:www.historycooperative.org/btw/index.html>

The Booker T. Washington Era
    <http:memory.loc.gov/ammem/aaohtml/exhibit/>

Up From Slavery: An Autobiography
    <http://xroads.virginia.edu/~HYPER/WASHINGTON/
    cover.html>

Index

Page numbers for photographs are in **boldface** type.

INDEX